Moody Press

A KING IS BORN

PATRICIA ST JOHN

Illustrated by Richard Scott

There was once a girl called Mary who lived in a little town set high on the top of a hill. When Mary climbed up to the flat roof of her house she could see miles and miles of green, fruitful countryside stretching away on every side, and, far away where the sun set, lay the sea.

Mary was a happy girl. She was going to marry Joseph the carpenter who lived in the same village. All her friends would come to her wedding feast, and Mary had many friends, for she was a kind, helpful girl and everyone loved her.

And then it happened! She was quite alone one day when suddenly she found that she was no longer by herself. The room seemed full of light, and a beautiful angel was in front of her.

At first Mary was frightened, but then the angel spoke. "Don't be afraid, Mary!" he said. "God is pleased with you. You are going to have a baby boy, and you must name Him Jesus. He will be a great king, and one day He will rule over the whole world."

"How can I have a baby?" asked Mary. "I'm not even married yet."

"This baby won't have an earthly father," said the angel. "He will be a special baby, and God will be His Father."

Mary wondered if anyone would believe this, but she did not argue. The angel spoke so gently that she felt quite safe. "I am ready for whatever God wants." she said.

Then Mary was left alone to think about the wonderful thing that was going to happen to her. God's very special baby was going to be born, and she was to be His mother.

I must tell Joseph, thought Mary.

But Joseph just couldn't believe her at first. It seemed so strange. He worked away in his carpenter's shop, sawing and hammering until the sky turned golden and it was too dark to work anymore. He lay down on his mattress and fell asleep, still wondering.

And then it happened again — the soft light and the voice of the angel with another message from God. "Don't worry, Joseph!" said the angel. "Mary is quite right. She is going to have a baby boy. But He won't have an earthly father because God will be His Father, and you must give Him a special name. You must name Him Jesus, because He is going to save His people from their sins."

Then Joseph woke up. The sun was rising, and the roosters were crowing all over the village of Nazareth. He felt happy for now he knew that everything was all right. Mary was a special girl, and the new baby was to be very special.

"God will certainly be with us," he said to himself as he opened his shop. But he didn't tell their secret to anyone. That was just for him and Mary.

It was nearly time for the baby to be born, when Emperor Augustus ordered everyone to go to the town or village where he had been born to be counted. Thousands of people set out, some on foot, some on donkeys or camels, and the roads were crowded with travellers. To make matters worse, it was winter; the nights were dark, the weather cold, and the roads muddy.

Mary and Joseph, who were now married, had to travel a long way, because Joseph had been born in the little town of Bethlehem, which was miles from Nazareth. It was a hard, tiring journey for Mary, who knew her baby might be born at any time.

Yet, as her donkey jogged along the hilly road, Mary was not afraid. Hundreds of years before, a man called Micah had written about God's special baby. He said that He would be born in Bethlehem. Now it was all coming true.

"It's all right, Joseph," said Mary. "My baby won't be born on the way. It was written that He will be born in Bethlehem, and to Bethlehem we shall come."

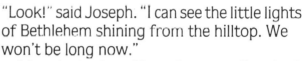

"Look!" said Joseph. "I can see the little lights of Bethlehem shining from the hilltop. We won't be long now."

Mary looked up. The other travellers had hurried ahead to find food and places to stay, but Mary could no longer be hurried, for she was tired out. It was quiet on the road under the stars, but when Joseph led the donkey in at the gates of the town, all was noise and bustle. The little stores were still open, and everyone was trying to buy food. Whole families camped on the street cooking over small fires.

Joseph looked around anxiously. "This way to the inn," he said. "Only a few minutes more, Mary, and you can lie down and rest."

When they reached the inn, Joseph knocked loudly on the door. The innkeeper's face appeared at an upper window. "It's my wife," Joseph explained. "Her baby is about to be born. Please, oh please, find us a corner!"

"Impossible!" replied the innkeeper. "The place is full up. Can't you see for yourself?" And he disappeared.

"Joseph, we must find somewhere quickly," said Mary. "My baby may be born any moment."

The street was nearly empty now. "There's an open doorway just ahead," said Joseph. "It seems to lead to a cave under the inn. We could go in there."

"Anywhere," said Mary.

They went in and Joseph lifted his lantern and looked around. It was a stone cave, and some cows were munching around a manger. But the air was warm with their milky breath, and Mary sank down on the straw. And there, in that stable, by lantern light, God's special baby was born.

It was a wonderful moment when Mary

heard His first cry and took Him in her arms. He looked like any other new baby, but Mary knew He was different. "Jesus the Savior," she murmured. "God here with us in the stable."

Joseph unpacked the long cloth they had brought and wrapped the baby in it like a small cocoon. "Where shall I lay Him?" he asked. "For you need to sleep."

"In the manger," whispered Mary. "There isn't anywhere else."

Everyone in Bethlehem slept as usual that night, and no one knew that God's own Son was lying there right in the midst of them — in a manger!

But outside the walls of Bethlehem the secret was known. A group of shepherds crouched around their fire on the hillside. For them the night had started quietly as usual. The sheep cropped the grass, and the shepherds pulled their cloaks around them and dozed. It was a dark, cold night.

Then suddenly one of them looked up and rubbed his eyes. Was he dreaming? He cried out, but the others had seen it too — a light much stronger than daylight shone round them. They covered their faces and huddled together, shaking with fear.

Then, out of the beautiful light, God's messenger spoke. "Don't be afraid!" he said. "I've come to give you good news, the most joyful news ever told. It's not only for you, it's for everybody, everywhere. Tonight in the town of Bethlehem a baby has been born, the Savior you have all been waiting for. And this is how you will know Him: you will find Him wrapped in a cloth and lying in a manger."

Then suddenly the light was no longer just

around them; it was everywhere, as though the starry sky had opened, pouring out light and beauty. In the golden glow there appeared crowds of joyful angels praising God. "Glory to God in the highest," they sang. "On earth peace and goodwill to men." It was the happiest music the shepherds had ever heard.

Then the light faded, and the music died away. The shepherds looked around. All was silent and dark, and the sheep grazed peacefully. Had it all been a dream?

"What shall we do?" the shepherds asked each other. They were no longer afraid — just amazed and joyful.

"We must go and see," said one.

"What about our sheep?" asked another.

They decided that the angel who had told them to go would certainly look after the sheep. So they set off together up the hill to the gates of Bethlehem. Fortunately, with so many travellers arriving at all hours, the gates had been left open. Nearly everyone was asleep by now, and the shepherds stood in the quiet street wondering where to go.

"Look!" whispered one. "Can you see a little light shining under that stable door below the inn? Let's look there."

Softly they opened the door. The place smelled of cattle, and a cow mooed softly. By the dim light of a lantern they could see a man lying asleep and a tired girl leaning against the manger. They crept forward, and there, nestled in straw, lay the baby they had come to find — wrapped in a cloth and lying in a manger, exactly as the angel had said.

They knelt and gazed at the child, and Joseph and Mary woke and knelt beside them. As they talked, the wonderful story was pieced together. "The angel said that this news was for everyone, everywhere," said the shepherds. "As soon as it's light we must start telling them."

At sunrise out they went into the streets, praising God and longing to share the news, although people found it hard to believe their story.

But Mary believed every word. She would never forget what the shepherds had told her, and she treasured it deep in her heart. This wonderful baby, welcomed by angels, was her baby — her own little son.

When Jewish babies were eight days old, they were taken to the Temple and dedicated to God. The parents had to take a lamb as a gift for the priest, or two pigeons if they were poor. "We'll take two pigeons, Mary," said Joseph. "That's all we can afford."

So they set out together on the long walk to the Temple at Jerusalem. It was a beautiful building, and many people were there, bringing big, expensive gifts. The priest hardly noticed the young couple carrying a new baby and two pigeons.

But there was someone who did notice. Simeon was a very old man, but he had prayed that he would not die until he had seen the Savior whom God had promised to send. Now God had answered his prayer. On that very day God told him to go to the Temple. Why today? he wondered as he climbed the steps.

He looked around and saw the little family, and suddenly he knew. He hurried across the courtyard, and Mary, looking into his face, knew too. She placed Jesus in Simeon's frail old arms.

"Lord," cried Simeon, "let me die content! I have seen the Savior, the light that will shine on our nation and on all the nations of the world."

He handed the baby back to Mary and blessed the young couple. Then he told them what God had said to him about Jesus. Mary and Joseph stood wondering, but old Simeon went away happy. He had seen all he had waited for, and now he was ready to go home to God.

Just about this time, far away in the lands beyond the sunrise, some very important people were setting out to visit Mary's little son. They were wise men who studied the stars, and they would often stand together on some hilltop or flat roof, watching the skies.

One night when the sun had set in the west, there, in the dark afterglow, they noticed a great, blazing star they had never seen before. "Something very important must have happened," said one of them.

"In the old Jewish books," said another, "it says that a mighty king will one day arise and save His nation. I think that time must have come, and the child has been born."

"Then we should go and visit Him," said a third. "Let's prepare gifts, load our camels, and get going."

"How shall we know the way?" asked the first.

"I think the star will lead us," said the second, and he was right. They started off towards the country of the Jews. As the sun was very hot during the day they rested. But every night at sunset, when the light faded above the sand and the palm trees, their beautiful star shone out. Then they loaded their camels and set out again by moonlight across the lonely desert. Sometimes foxes and hyenas barked, and desert lions roared, but they were not afraid. They knew their star would lead them safely to the new king.

At last, at last! The sun, rising behind them, showed them high mountains far away in the distance, and among those mountains lay the royal city of Jerusalem.

"We needn't wait till night for the star to show us the way," said one of the wise men. "The great king could only be born in the palace."

All day they climbed until they reached the great gates of the city. Then they hurried through the crowded streets to the entrance of the palace, where a sentry stood on duty.

"Please take us to the king," said the wise men. "We have travelled far to bring presents for the royal baby."

"Baby?" said the sentry. "There's no baby here!" But he saw they were men of importance, so he took them in to see King Herod.

"The promised king of the Jews has certainly been born," said the wise men. "We have seen His star in the east."

Herod pretended to be very pleased, but inside he was frightened. Another king? he thought. Then what is to become of me?

He sent for his own wise men. "Everyone has heard about this great king who is going to be born," he said to them. "Look in the old books and see if it says where."

"The old books say He will be born in Bethlehem," said Herod's wise men.

The king turned to his puzzled visitors. "I'm afraid you've made a mistake," he said. "The great king is to be born in Bethlehem. Go and look for Him there, and, when you find Him, come back and tell me. I would like to take Him a present too."

But under his breath he muttered: "And I shall kill Him as soon as possible!"

Sunset again — but this time the wise men watched carefully. Sure enough, as the sky darkened, their beautiful star rose above the hills. And, sure enough, it was leading them south.

It was only a short journey to Bethlehem, and how glad they were to lie down and sleep. Next morning they woke before dawn.

"I had such a strange dream," said the first.

"So did I," said the second.

"And I did too," said the third.

"God spoke to me," said the first. "He said: *'Don't go back to Herod*!'"

"And that's just what he said to us," said the others. "We must find the child and go back another way."

It was easy to find the house where Joseph, Mary, and Jesus were living, for the star had stopped right over it and shone its bright beams on the flat roof. Jesus had grown into a toddler by now, and Mary was used to people noticing Him. All the same, she was quite surprised when these strangers in fine clothes knocked at her door.

But they did not need to explain. As soon as they saw the child, their faces lit up with joy. They knelt down and unpacked their rich gifts — gold and beautiful perfumes of frankincense and myrrh. They did not mind at all that it was only a poor little house, because they had found Jesus.

Then, while Herod sat in his palace waiting impatiently for them to come back, the wise men started home by another way, with empty packs and happy hearts. They had found all they wanted to find, forever.

"Wake up, Mary! Wrap up Jesus and collect some clothes! I've filled the waterpot and packed what food we have, and the gifts of those wise men. Come quickly; there isn't a moment to lose!"

"But Joseph, whatever's the matter? It's the middle of the night!"

"I know. But I've had a terrible dream. Herod will try to kill Jesus. Even now his soldiers may be on the road. God has warned us to run away."

"But where are we going?"

"South, to Egypt. We dare not go north; we might meet them."

So when Herod's soldiers rode into Bethlehem with orders to kill every baby under two years old, the one baby he really wanted was already safely on the road. God was looking after His son, and no one could touch Him till God's time came.

Joseph, Mary, and Jesus stayed in Egypt for several years. It was a hot, flat, dusty country, and sometimes when the day's work was done they would sit and watch the sun set over the river, and perhaps Jesus would say, "Mother, tell me about home."

Then Mary would talk about the beautiful country of hills and valleys and streams that they had left behind, and Jesus would say, "Shall we ever go back?" And Mary would answer sadly, "I don't know, son. God will tell us."

But one morning Joseph woke them early. He was happy and excited. "Get up," he said. "We must start packing at once. We're going home."

"But Joseph," said Mary, "are you sure? Is it really safe?"

"Yes," said Joseph. "It's quite safe. Once again an angel came in my dreams and told me that the wicked King Herod is dead, and we can go back to Nazareth."

So they set out again on the long journey across the desert. But this time Mary wasn't afraid. She was going home. Early one morning a few weeks later, she suddenly said, "Look, Jesus! Can you see that little white town on the hilltop, shining in the sunrise? That's Nazareth, and we've come home!"

And there, in that little house behind the carpenter's shop, Jesus grew to be a man. And because He was God's son, God's goodness and beauty shone through Him and everybody loved Him.

You can find the story of the birth of Jesus in your Bible.

The story of the angel's message to Mary is in Luke 1:26–38.
The story of Joseph's dream is in Matthew 1:18–25.
The story of the birth of Jesus in Bethlehem is in Luke 2:1–7.
The story of the shepherds is in Luke 2:8–20.
The story of Simeon blessing the baby is in Luke 2:22–38.
The story of the wise men is in Matthew 2:1–12.
The story of the journey to Egypt and back is in Matthew 2:13–23.